The Three Best THINGS

An Illustrated Selection of
• IRISH TRIADS •

Introduction by
Fergus Kelly

Illustrated by Aislinn Adams

Appletree Press

First published in 1993 by
The Appletree Press Ltd
19-21 Alfred Street
Belfast BT2 8DL

© Appletree Press, 1993

British Library Cataloguing-in-Publication Data
A catalogue record for this book is
available from the British Library.

ISBN 0 86281 376 X

Printed in the EC.

9 8 7 6 5 4 3 2 1

Introduction

The arrangement of ideas in groups of three is natural and convenient, and consequently we find examples of the triad form in practically all recorded literatures, both oral and written. Among the Celtic-speaking peoples, triads seem to have been particularly popular, and they feature prominently in the native oral traditions of Ireland, Scotland, Wales and Brittany. Many of these triads are witty, with an amusing climax – or anticlimax – in the third item. The technique can be illustrated by quoting a Scottish Gaelic triad of the last century: 'The three most pleasant things which ever happened to me: my mother, my home and my purse.'

In many Irish triads of the same period, there are humorous jibes at female behaviour – or in some cases at male inability to cope with it. Again, the third item may be an anticlimax, as in the following example: 'There are three kinds of men who fail to understand women: young men, old men and middle-aged men.' Mothers-in-law are the target of a triad recorded from oral tradition in many parts of Ireland: 'The three sharpest things in the world: the eye of a cat after a mouse, the eye of a mason after a stone, the eye of a mother-in-law after her daughter-in-law.'

Moving further back in time, we witness a similar rich tradition of triads in the early manuscripts of Ireland and Wales. The principal Welsh collection is found in thirteenth- and fourteenth-century manuscripts, but it contains triads which are many centuries older. The principal Irish collection – from which the present selection has been made – dates from about the ninth century. It contains 214 triads, as well as some duads (two items), tetrads (four items) and nonads (nine items). A translation of the complete collection was published by the great German scholar Kuno Meyer in 1906, but is long out of print. A new edition is in the course of preparation at the School of Celtic Studies, Dublin Institute for Advanced Studies.

Some of these triads may come from ninth-century oral tradition, but in general this is a literary composition, probably most of it the work of a single author. His aim is to describe various aspects of life as he sees it around him. Sometimes there is no implied moral in his observations: he is merely a neutral recorder of some natural or human phenomenon. But more often he adopts a particular ethical standpoint and uses the triad form to express his disapproval of vices, such as anger, lust, gluttony and laziness. He is especially concerned to castigate breaches of good manners or etiquette. We can thus learn from him how a person was expected to behave in polite society in ninth-century Ireland! In contrast to some of the triads of more recent folk tradition, his triads in general display respect for a woman's point of view. Indeed, one of the triads quoted in this selection encapsulates in a remarkably sympathetic and sensitive way the lot of a wife: 'Three drops of a married woman: a drop of blood, a tear-drop, a drop of sweat.'

Like many moralists, the author's observations are sometimes rather banal, but he can also be incisive and profound. He is particularly skilled at juxtaposing images from the natural world alongside some aspect of human behaviour, as in: 'Three wealths in barren places: a well in a mountain, fire out of a stone, wealth in the possession of a mean man.'

Technically, these triads display a number of interesting points. The triad which I have just quoted is an example of one of the author's favourite devices: the use of paradox. In this case, he is clearly fascinated by the paradox that two life-giving elements – water and fire – can reside in the seemingly lifeless environment of a mountain or a stone. He links these ideas with a further paradox: the wealthy man who is too mean to benefit anybody with his wealth. Another device which the author relishes is the arrangement of his triads in contrasting pairs. This feature can be seen in some of the triads in the present selection. For example, 'Three youthful sisters' is followed by 'Three aged sisters'.

I have no doubt that modern readers will find this well-chosen selection of Irish triads both entertaining and thought-provoking.

Fergus Kelly

Three things that are best in the world:

the hand of a good carpenter,
the hand of a skilled woman,
the hand of a good smith.

Three rejoicings followed by sorrow:

a wooer's,
a thief's,
a tale-bearer's.

Three rejoicings that are worse than sorrow:

the joy of a man who has defrauded another,
the joy of a man who has perjured himself,
the joy of a man who has slain his brother
in contesting his land.

Three unfortunate things for a householder:

proposing to a bad woman,
serving a bad chief,
exchanging for bad land.

Three excellent things for a householder:

proposing to a good woman,
serving a good chief,
exchanging for good land.

Three things which justice demands:

judgement,
measure,
conscience.

Three things which judgement demands:

wisdom,
penetration,
knowledge.

Three things for which an enemy is loved:

wealth,
beauty,
worth.

Three things for which a friend is hated:

trespassing,
keeping aloof,
fecklessness.

Three rude ones of the world:

a youngster mocking an old man,
a healthy person mocking an invalid,
a wise man mocking a fool.

Three sparks that kindle love:

a face,
demeanour,
speech.

Three deposits with usufruct:

depositing a woman,
a horse,
salt.

Three glories of the gathering:

a beautiful wife,
a good horse,
a swift hound.

Three ungentlemanly things:

interrupting stories,
a mischievous game,
jesting so as to raise a blush.

Three smiles that are worse than sorrow:

the smile of the snow as it melts,
the smile of your wife on you
after another man has been with her,
the grin of a hound ready to leap at you.

Three fewnesses that are better than plenty:

a fewness of fine words,
a fewness of cows in grass,
a fewness of friends around ale.

Three laughing-stocks of the world:

an angry man,
a jealous man,
a niggard.

Three ruins of a tribe:

a lying chief,
a false judge,
a lustful priest.

Three preparations of a good man's house:

ale,
a bath,
a large fire.

Three characteristics of obstinacy:

long visits,
staring,
constant questioning.

Three signs of a fop:

the track of his comb in his hair,
the track of his teeth in his food,
the track of his stick behind him.

Three maidens that bring love to good fortune:

silence,
diligence,
sincerity.

Three maidens that bring hatred upon misfortune:

talking,
laziness,
insincerity.

The three chief sins:

avarice,
gluttony,
lust.

Three things that constitute a buffoon:

blowing out his cheek,
blowing out his satchel,
blowing out his belly.

Three things that constitute a harper:

a tune to make you cry,
a tune to make you laugh,
a tune to put you to sleep.

Three drops of a wedded woman:

a drop of blood,
a tear-drop,
a drop of sweat.

Three false sisters:

'perhaps',
'maybe',
'I dare say'.

Three sounds of increase:

the lowing of a cow in milk,
the din of a smithy,
the swish of a plough.

Three things by which
every angry person is known:

an outburst of passion,
trembling,
growing pale.

Three things that characterise
every patient person:

repose,
silence,
blushing.

Three signs of folly:

contention,
wrangling,
attachment to everybody.

Three candles that illumine every darkness:

truth,
nature,
knowledge.

Three things that make a fool wise:

learning,
steadiness,
docility.

Three things that make a wise man foolish:

quarrelling,
anger,
drunkenness.

Three things that show every good man:

a special gift,
valour,
piety.

Three things that show a bad man:

bitterness,
hatred,
cowardice.

Three things that constitute a king:

a contract with other kings,
the feast of Tara,
abundance during his reign.

Three inheritances that are divided
in the presence of heirs:

the inheritance of a jester,
of a madman,
and of an old man.

Three youthful sisters:

   desire,
   beauty,
   generosity.

Three aged sisters:

groanings,
chastity,
ugliness.

Three woman-days:

Monday,
Tuesday,
Wednesday.

If women go to men on those days, the men will love them better
than they the men, and the women will survive the men.

48

Mon
Tue
Wed
Thur
Fri
Sat
Sun

Three man-days:

Thursday,
Friday,
Sunday.

If women go to men on those days, they will not be loved, and
their husbands will survive them. Saturday, however, is a common
day. It is equally lucky to them. Monday is a free day to
undertake any business.

Three things that are undignified for everyone:

driving one's horse before one's lord
so as to soil his dress,
going to speak to him without being summoned,
staring in his face as he is eating his food.

Three welcomes of an ale-house:

plenty,
kindliness,
art.

Three whose spirits are highest:

a young scholar after having read his psalms,
a youngster who has put on a man's attire,
a maiden who has been made a woman.

Three prohibitions of food:

to eat it without giving thanks,
to eat it before its proper time,
to eat it after a guest.

Three things that are best for a chief:

justice,
peace,
an army.

Three things that are worst for a chief:

sloth,
treachery,
evil counsel.

Three indications of dignity in a person:

a fine figure,
a fine bearing,
eloquence.

Three coffers whose depth is not known:

the coffer of a chieftain,
of the Church,
of a privileged poet.

Three disagreeable things at home:

a scolding wife,
a squalling child,
a smokey chimney.

The three finest sights in the world:

a field of ripe wheat,
a ship in full sail,
and the wife of a MacDonnell with child.